Booklet by:

Daniel S. Merritt

contact – danielsmerritt@yahoo.com

youtube - Daniel S Merritt

facebook - Daniel Merritt

https://raccoon301smith.wixsite.com/merrittmorsels

Copyright September 2004 - Revised August 2024

ISBN: 978-1-965789-90-2

4
CONTENTS

A CHRONOLOGICAL BIBLE READING STUDY GUIDE

A Study Guide with Questions
and Some Useful Information on God's

Holy Bible

BY:
DANIEL S. (STEVE) MERRITT

I accepted Jesus as Lord in 1954, by believing in Him (John 3:16), repenting of my sins (Acts 2:38), confessing Jesus as God's Son (Romans 10:9), and was immersed into Christ (Galatians 3:27), and to wash away my sins (Acts 22:16), and to receive the Holy Spirit (Acts 2:38). Then I read, that I needed to be 'faithful unto death'. Through Bible study, I learned what our Lord requires (Galatians 5:16-26). This was not all, but enough to give me a good start; but I needed to study more.

From my youth, I thought about becoming a preacher, but did not want to go to college. After High School, I became a printer which I enjoyed. My wife and I continued serving our Lord, all through life. Marrying a Christian was important to us. In 1980, my brother convinced me to go to Bible college. Having 'matured' some, I did attend Johnson Bible College, earning a BA in Bible and Preaching. I ministered for several churches, including nine years in Germany, ministering to our Military.

Much later, I wanted to read the Bible in chronological order. I could not find one that I liked, so between 2002 and 2004, I made one. I spent much time researching dates, and other information that would help me in achieving my goal. There were questions that I had, so I put them in this booklet, with Scriptures. These are questions that I know others have as well. One of my goals, was to encourage Bible reading and study. I pray others will use this book to have a closer walk with our Lord.

Grace to you and peace from God our Father
and the Lord Jesus Christ

"For as many things as were written before were written for our instruction, that we through the endurance and encouragement of the Scriptures might have hope." *Romans 15:4*

"All Scripture is God inspired, and is profitable for teaching, for persuasion, for correction for discipline, which is in righteousness, that the man of God may be complete, fully fitted for every good work." *II Timothy 3:16-17*

"Be ever studying to present yourself approved to God, a workman who does not need to be ashamed, teaching accurately the Word of Truth." *II Timothy 2:15*

(Translated from the Greek)

Daily Bible Reading In (sort of) Chronological Order

(All Scholars do not agree on all the dates, and those listed are approximate.) Use a pencil and mark off each chapter as you read it.

Old Testament

Genesis 1, 2, 3, 4, 5, 6, 7, 8, 9, 10 – *Creation through 1446 BC*

Job 1, 2, 3, 4, 5, 6, 7, 8, 9, 10, 11, 12, 13, 14, 15, 16, 17, 18, 19 20, 21, 22, 23, 24, 25, 26, 27, 28, 29, 30, 31, 32, 33, 34, 35, 36, 37, 38, 39, 40, 41, 42 – *Between 2000 and 1800 BC*

Genesis 11, 12, 13, 14, 15, 16, 17, 18, 19, 20, 21, 22, 23, 24, 25, 26, 27, 28, 29, 30, 31, 32, 33, 34, 35, 36, 37, 38, 39, 40, 41, 42, 43, 44, 45, 46, 47, 48, 49, 50

Exodus 1, 2, 3, 4, 5, 6, 7, 8, 9, 10, 11, 12, 13, 14, 15, 16, 17, 18, 19, 20, 21, 22, 23, 24, 25, 26, 27, 28, 29, 30, 31, 32, 33, 34, 35, 36, 37, 38, 39, 40 – *Between 1446 and 1406 BC*

Leviticus 1, 2, 3, 4, 5, 6, 7, 8, 9, 10, 11, 12, 13, 14, 15, 16, 17, 18, 19, 20, 21, 22, 23, 24, 25, 26, 27

Numbers 1, 2, 3, 4, 5, 6, 7, 8, 9, 10, 11, 12, 13, 14, 15, 16, 17, 18,19, 20, 21, 22, 23, 24, 25, 26, 27, 28, 29, 30, 31, 32, 33, 34, 35, 36

Deuteronomy 1, 2, 3, 4, 5, 6, 7, 8, 9, 10, 11, 12, 13, 14, 15, 16, 17, 18, 19, 20, 21, 22, 23, 24, 25, 26, 27, 28, 29, 30, 31, 32, 33, 34

Joshua 1, 2, 3, 4, 5, 6, 7, 8, 9, 10, 11, 12, 13, 14, 15, 16, 17, 18, 19, 20, 21, 22, 23, 24 – *1405-1390 BC*

Judges 1, 2, 3, 4, 5, 6, 7, 8, 9, 10, 11, 12, 13, 14, 15, 16, 17

NOTES:

Ruth 1, 2, 3, 4 — *1278 BC*
Judges 18, 19, 20, 21 — *1380-1045 BC*

I Samuel 1, 2, 3, 4, 5, 6, 7, 8, 9, 10, 11, 12, 13, 14, 15, 16, 17, 18, 19, 20, 21, 22, 23, 24, 25, 26, 27, 28, 29, 30 (Samuel – *1075-1035 BC*, Saul – *1054-1011 BC*, David – *1011-971 BC*)

I Chronicles 1, 2, 3, 4, 5, 6, 7, 8, 9—(2 ½ tribes taken to Assyria)

I Samuel 31 and **I Chronicles** 10 (Saul Killed)

II Samuel 1, 2, 3, 4 (David made king of Judah; Abner joins David)

II Samuel 5:1-10 and **I Chronicles** 11:1-9 (David Anointed King)

I Chronicles 12

II Samuel 5:11-25 and **I Chronicles** 14 (War with Philistia)

II Samuel 6:1-11 and **I Chronicles** 13 (Moving Ark Wrong)

II Samuel 6:12-16, 20-23 and **I Chronicles** 15 (Moving Ark right/Wife)

II Samuel 6:17-19 and **I Chronicles** 16 (Sacrifices to God)

II Samuel 7 and **I Chronicles** 17 (David's Desire)

II Samuel 8, 9, 10 and **I Chronicles** 18, 19 (David's Victories)

II Samuel 11, 12 and I **Chronicles** 20:1-3 (David &Bathsheba)

II Samuel 13, 14, 15, 16, 17, 18, 19, 20, 21:1-14 (Absalom's Revolt)

II Samuel 21:15-22 and **I Chronicles** 20:4-8 (Killing Goliath's brother)

II Samuel 22, 23:1-7 (David's Song to the Lord)

9
NOTES:

II Samuel 23:8-39 and **I Chronicles** 11:10-47 (David's Mighty Men)

II Samuel 24 and **I Chronicles** 21 (David Numbers Israel)

Psalms 1, 2, 3, 4, 5, 6, 7, 8, 9, 10, 11, 12, 13, 14, 15, 16, 17, 18, 19, 20, 21, 22, 23, 24, 25, 26, 27, 28, 29, 30, 31, 32, 33, 34, 35, 36, 37, 38, 39, 40, 41, 42, 43, 44, 45, 46, 47, 48, 49, 50, 51, 52, 53, 54, 55, 56, 57, 58, 59, 60, 61, 62, 63, 64, 65, 66, 67, 68, 69, 70, 71, 72, 73, 74, 75, 76, 77, 78, 79, 80, 81, 82, 83, 84, 85, 86, 87, 88, 89, 90, 91, 92, 93, 94, 95, 96, 97, 98, 99, 100, 101, 102, 103, 104, 105, 106, 107, 108, 109, 110, 111, 112, 113, 114, 115, 116, 117, 118, 119, 120, 121, 122, 123, 124, 125, 126, 127, 128, 129, 130, 131, 132, 133, 134, 135, 136, 137, 138, 139, 140, 141, 142, 143, 144, 145, 146, 147, 148, 149, 150

I Kings 1, 2:1-9 and **I Chronicles** 22 (Instructions to Solomon)

I Chronicles 23, 24, 25, 26, 27, 28, 29:1-25

I Kings 2:10-11 and **I Chronicles** 29:26-30 (David Dies)

I Kings 2:12-46, 3, 4, 5 and **II Chronicles** 1, 2 – _971-931 BC_ (Solomon – About 480 Years Since Exodus)

I Kings 6, 7, 8 and **II Chronicles** 3, 4, 5, 6, 7:1-11

I Kings 9, 10, 11 and **II Chronicles** 7:12-22, 8, 9

Proverbs 1, 2, 3, 4, 5, 6, 7, 8, 9, 10, 11, 12, 13, 14, 15, 16, 17, 18, 19, 20, 21, 22, 23, 24, 25, 26, 27, 28, 29, 30, 31

Ecclesiastes 1, 2, 3, 4, 5, 6, 7, 8, 9, 10, 11, 12

Song of Solomon 1, 2, 3, 4, 5, 6, 7, 8

NOTES:

The Kingdom divided into Judah and Israel
(931 BC)

I **Kings** 12, 13, 14 and II **Chronicles** 10, 11, 12

I **Kings** 15, 16:1-28 and II Chronicles 13, 14, 15, 16

I **Kings** 16:29-34; 17, 18, 19, 20, 21, 22 II **Chronicles** 17, 18, 19, 20, 21, 22:1-9 (Elijah)

In Judah

- Rehoboam - *931-913 BC*
- Abijah - *913-911 BC*
- Asa - *911-869 BC*
- Jehoshaphat - *870-848 BC*;

In Israel

- Jeroboam I - *931-910 BC*
- Nadab - *910-909 BC*
- Baasha - *909-886 BC*
- Elah - *886-885 BC*
- Zimri – *885 BC*
- Tibni - *885-880 BC*
- Omri – *880-874 BC*
- Ahab - *874-853 BC*
- Ahaziah - *853-852 BC*

II **Kings** 1, 2, 3, 4, 5, 6, 7, 8, 9:1-29 — *852-841 BC*

In Judah

- Jehoram – *848-841 BC*
- Ahaziah – *841 BC*

In Israel

- Jehoram/Joram – *852-841 BC* (Elisha)

Obadiah 1 – *847 BC* (Israel and Edom)

13
NOTES:

II Kings 9:30-37, 10 (Jehu, king of Israel) _841-814 BC_

Joel 1, 2, 3 – _835-815 BC_ (Judah)

II Kings 11, 12, 13, 14 – _841-753 BC_
In Judah

- Athaliah – _841-835 BC_
- Jehoash/Joash – _835-796_
- Amaziah – _796-767 BC;_

In Israel

- Jehoahaz – _814-798 BC_
- Jehoash/Joash – _798-782 BC_
- Jeroboam II – _782-753 BC_

II Chronicles 22:10-12, 23, 24, 25 and **Jonah** 1, 2, 3, 4 – _760 BC_
(Nineveh)

Amos 1, 2, 3, 4, 5, 6, 7, 8, 9 — _760-753 BC_ (Israel)

II Kings 15, 16, 17 and **II Chronicles** 26, 27, 28 — _753-722 BC_
In Judah

- Uzziah/Azariah - _767-740 BC_
- Jotham - _740-731 BC_
- Jehoahaz/Ahaz - _732-716 BC_

In Israel

- Zechariah - _753-752 BC_
- Shallun – _752 BC_
- Menahem _752-742 BC_
- Pekahiah - _742-740 BC_
- Pekeh - _740-732 BC_
- Hoshea - _732-722 BC_

Hosea 1, 2, 3, 4, 5, 6, 7, 8, 9, 10,11, 12, 13, 14 — _753-710 BC_

15
NOTES:

Micah 1, 2, 3, 4, 5, 6, 7 -- _735-710 BC_ (Judah and Israel)

Fall of Northern Kingdom (Israel)
(722 BC)

Isaiah 1, 2, 3, 4, 5, 6, 7, 8, 9, 10, 11, 12, 13, 14, 15, 16, 17, 18, 19, 20, 21, 22, 23, 24, 25, 26, 27, 28, 29, 30, 31, 32, 33, 34, 35,-- _740-700 BC_ (Judah)

II Kings 18 and **II Chronicles** 29, 30 and **Isaiah** 36 (Hezekiah) _716-686 BC_

II Kings 19, 20 and **II Chronicles** 31, 32 and **Isaiah** 37, 38, 39

II Kings 21 and **II Chronicles** 33

- Manasseh – _687-642 BC_
- Amon – _642-640 BC_

Isaiah 40, 41, 42, 43, 44, 45, 46, 47, 48, 49, 50, 51, 52, 53, 54, 55, 56, 57, 58, 59, 60, 61, 62, 63, 64, 65, 66

Nahum 1, 2, 3 — _640 BC_ (In Judah against Nineveh)

Zephaniah 1, 2, 3 –— _640-612 BC_ (Judah)

II Kings 22, 23:1-33 and **II Chronicles** 34, 35, 36:1-3

- Josiah - _640-609 BC_
- Jehoahaz II – _609 BC_

Jeremiah 1, 2, 3, 4, 5, 6, 7, 8, 9, 10, 11, 12, 13, 14, 15, 16, 17, 18, 19, 20, 21, 22, 23, 24, 25, 26 — _627-605 BC_ (Jerusalem)

Habakkuk 1, 2, 3 — _610 BC_ (Judah)

NOTES:

II Kings 23:34-37, 24:1-7 and **II Chronicles** 36:4-8 (Jehoiakim/Eliakim) — _609-597 BC_ — (1st Babylonian captivity – 3,023 taken captive. See Jeremiah 52:28-30; II Kings 24:11-16)

Daniel 1, 2, 3 — _605-539 BC_ (Babylon)

II Kings 24:8-16 and **II Chronicles** 36:9-10 (Jehoiachin/ Jeconiah) — _597 BC_ — (2nd Babylonian captivity — 832 taken captive. See Jeremiah 52:28-30. Plus another 8,000)

Ezekiel 1, 2, 3, 4, 5, 6, 7, 8, 9, 10, 11, 12, 13, 14, 15, 16, 17, 18, 19, 20, 21, 22, 23, 24, 25, 26, 27, 28, 29, 30, 31, 32, 33, 34, 35, 36, 37, 38, 39, 40, 41, 42, 43, 44, 45, 46, 47, 48 — _592-570 BC_

Jeremiah 27, 28, 29, 30, 31, 32, 33, 34, 35, 36, 37, 38, 39:1-10, 52:1-30 — _605-586 BC_

II Kings 24:17-20, 25:1-21 (Zedekiah/Mattaniah) — _597-587 BC_ — (3rd Babylonian captivity. 745 taken captive; plus thousands more — II Kings 24:11-16)

Fall of Southern Kingdom (Judah)
(586 BC)

II Kings 25:22-26 — _586-582 BC_ — Gedaliah

Lamentations 1, 2, 3, 4, 5 — _586 BC_

Jeremiah 39:11-18, 40, 41, 42, 43, 44, 45, 46, 47, 48, 49, 50, 51, — _586-580 BC_

II Kings 25:27-30 and **II Chronicles** 36:11-21 and **Jeremiah** 52:31-34 — _560 BC_ — (Release of Jehoiachin in Babylon)

NOTES:

Daniel 4, 5, 6, 7, 8, 9, 10, 11, 12 — *539-536 BC* (Medes & Persians take Babylon)

- Chap. 1 written in Hebrew
- Chapters 2-7 written in Aramaic – future of Gentiles
- Chapters 8-12 written in Hebrew – future of Jews under Gentiles

II Chronicles 36:22-23 and **Ezra** 1, 2, 3, 4, 5, 6 — *538-516 BC* (First Return to Jerusalem by Remnant by Cyrus' Decree)

Haggai 1, 2 — *520 BC* (To remnant in Judah)

Zechariah 1, 2, 3, 4, 5, 6, 7, 8, 9 — *520-518 BC* (Remnant)

Esther 1, 2, 3, 4, 5, 6, 7, 8, 9, 10 — *Between Ezra 6 and 7* (Exiles)

Zechariah 10, 11, 12, 13, 14 — *480-470 BC (Remnant)*

Ezra 7, 8, 9, 10 -- *458-457 BC* (Second return to Jerusalem)

Nehemiah 1, 2, 3, 4, 5, 6, 7, 8, 9, 10, 11, 12, 13 — *444-425 BC* (Wall Rebuilt 444 BC. Third return to Jerusalem by Remnant)

Malachi 1, 2, 3, 4 — *432-425 BC* (Remnant in Judah)

Other religious leaders in other places:

- (Buddha – 560-480 BC in India)
- (Confucius – 551-479 BC in China)
- (Socrates – 470-399 BC in Greece)
- (Muhammad – 569-632 AD in Arabia)

SPECIAL STUDY:
THE TWO <u>LOVES</u> IN THE NEW TESTAMENT

<u>LOVE (loves, loved)</u> - *Phileo* - about 32 times in the NT. Distinguished from *agapao* in that it more nearly represents 'tender affection' or sometimes 'desire.'

Never used in a command to men to love God.

1. *Matthew 6:5* – Hypocrites **love** to pray standing...
2. *Matthew 23:6* – Scribes & Pharisees **love** the best places
3. *Luke 20:46*   Scribes...**love** the best places
4. *John 11:3*   Lord, behold, he whom You **love** is sick
5. *John 15:19*   the world would **love** its own
6. *John 21:15* You know that I **love** You
7. *John* 21:16   You know that I **love** You
8. *John*   21:17   son of Jonah, do you **love** Me
9. *John*   21:17   do you **love** Me
10. *John* 21:17 You know that I **love** You
11. *Romans 12:10* affectionate to one another with brotherly **love**
12. *I Corinthians 16:22*   if anyone does not **love** the Lord Jesus
13. *I Thessalonians 4:9*   but concerning brotherly **love**
14. *I Timothy 6:10* for the **love** of money
15. *Titus 2:4*   admonish the young women to **love** their...
16. *Titus 2:4*   to **love** their children
17. *Titus*   3:4   and the **love** of God our Savior toward man
18. *Titus* 3:15   greet those who **love** in the faith
19. *Hebrews 13:1* let brotherly **love** continue
20. *I Peter 1:22*   the Spirit in sincere **love** of the brethren
21. *I Peter 3:8* **love** as brothers
22. *Revelation 3:19* as many as I **love**, I rebuke and chasten

LOVED

23. *John 11:36* Jews said, see how He **loved** him
24. *John 16:27* because you have **loved** Me
25. *John 20:2* the other disciple whom Jesus **loved**

26. *Matthew 10:37* he who **loves** father or mother more than Me
27. *Matthew 10:37* who **loves** son or daughter more than Me is not worthy of Me
28. *John 5:20* for the Father **loves** the Son
29. *John 12:25* he who **loves** his life will lose it
30. *John 16:27* for the Father Himself **loves** you
31. *III John 9* but Diotrephes who **loved** to have the...
32. *Revelation 22:15* but outside are dogs...and whoever **loves** and practices a lie

All Other Words For LOVE Are *AGAPAO* – Or Derivatives used over 200 times in NT (W. E. Vine)

Presents the characteristic word of Christianity, and since the Spirit of revelation has used it to express ideas previously unknown, inquiry into its use, whether in Greek literature or in the Septuagint, throws but little light upon its distinctive meaning in the NT.

Christian love has God for its primary object, and expresses itself first of all in implicit obedience to His commandments.

Christian love, toward the brethren, or men generally, is not an impulse from feelings, it does not run with the natural inclinations, nor does it spend itself only upon those for whom some affinity is discovered. Love seeks the welfare of all, and works no ill to any; love seeks opportunity to do good to all men, and especially them that are of the household of faith.

THE FRUIT OF THE SPIRIT

"I say then: Walk in the Spirit, and you shall not fulfill the lust of the flesh. . .

But the fruit of the Spirit is love, joy, peace, longsuffering, kindness, goodness, faithfulness, gentleness, self-control. Against such there is no law. And those who are Christ's have crucified the flesh with its passions and desires. If we live in the Spirit, let us also walk in the Spirit."

Galatians 5:16, 22-25, <u>New King James Version</u>

See also: Colossians 3:12-17; **Philippians** 4:4-9; **John** 15:1-17; **Romans** 8:1-11; **Matthew** 25:31-46

New Testament in the Order It was Written

Matthew 1, 2, 3, 4, 5, 6, 7, 8, 9, 10, 11, 12, 13, 14, 15, 16, 17, 18, 19, 20, 21, 22, 23, 24, 25, 26, 27, 28 — 4 BC-33 AD - Written mid 40's AD

Acts 1, 2, 3, 4, 5, 6, 7, 8, 9, 10, 11, 12 — 33 AD - (The Early Church - Peter and John)

James 1, 2, 3, 4, 5 — Written 44-45 AD

Acts 13, 14 — 46-48 AD - (1st Missionary Journey)

Galatians 1, 2, 3, 4, 5, 6 — 48 AD

Acts 15:1-35 - (Paul in Antioch)

Acts 15:36-41, 16, 17, 18:1-22 — 50-52 AD - (2nd Missionary Journey)

I Thessalonians 1, 2, 3, 4, 5 — 51 AD

II Thessalonians 1, 2, 3 — 51 AD

Acts 18:23-28, 19, 20, 21:1-16 — 53-58 AD - (3rd Missionary Journey)

I Corinthians 1, 2, 3, 4, 5, 6, 7, 8, 9, 10, 11, 12, 13, 14, 15, 16 — 56 AD

II Corinthians 1, 2, 3, 4, 5, 6, 7, 8, 9, 10, 11, 12, 13 — 56 AD

Romans 1, 2, 3, 4, 5, 6, 7, 8, 9, 10, 11, 12, 13, 14, 15, 16 — 56-57 AD

Acts 21:17-40, 22, 23, 24, 25, 26 — 58-59 AD - (Paul's Arrest, Trials, & Prison)

NOTES:

Luke 1, 2, 3, 4, 5, 6, 7, 8, 9, 10, 11, 12, 13, 14, 15, 16, 17, 18, 19, 20, 21, 22, 23, 24 — Written 58-60 AD

(Acts written around 62 AD)

Acts 27, 28 — 60-62 AD — (Trip to Rome and Prison)

Ephesians 1, 2, 3, 4, 5, 6 — 60 AD

Mark 1, 2, 3, 4, 5, 6, 7, 8, 9, 10, 11, 12, 13, 14, 15, 16 — 60 AD

Colossians 1, 2, 3, 4 — 61 AD

Philemon 1 — 61 AD

Philippians 1, 2, 3, 4 — 62 AD

(Paul may have been set free)

I Timothy 1, 2, 3, 4, 5, 6 — 62 AD

I Peter 1, 2, 3, 4, 5 — 64 AD

II Peter 1, 2, 3 — 64 AD

Titus 1, 2, 3 — 66 AD

John 1, 2, 3, 4, 5, 6, 7, 8, 9, 10, 11, 12, 13, 14, 15, 16, 17, 18, 19, 20, 21 — 65-70 AD

(Possible Second Imprisonment)

II Timothy 1, 2, 3, 4 — 67 AD

Hebrews 1, 2, 3, 4, 5, 6, 7, 8, 9, 10, 11, 12, 13 — 66-69 AD

Jude 1 — 66-75 AD

NOTES:

I John 1, 2, 3, 4, 5 — 65-68 AD

II John 1 — 65-68 AD

III John 1 — 65-68 AD

Revelation 1, 2, 3, 4, 5, 6, 7, 8, 9, 10, 11, 12, 13, 14, 15, 16, 17, 18, 19, 20, 21, 22

65-68 AD – Many believe this to be the date Revelation was written. If so, the letter tells of the destruction of Jerusalem and the temple by the Roman army, and the end of the Jewish nation. John did say that these events must shortly take place, and that the time was at hand and near: 1:1, 3; 22:6, 10. Believed by:

- Papias (first century)
- the Muratorian Cannon (170 AD)
- Clement (150-215)
- Epiphanius of Salamis (315-403)
- Sir Isaac Newton (1733)
- F.W. Farrar (1831-1904)
- Robert Jamieson of Jamieson, Fausset, Brown (1871)
- Philip Schaff (1877)
- Robert Young (late 1800's)
- George Ladd (1972)
- John A.T. Robertson (1976)
- A.N. Wilson (1977)
- Steve Gregg (1997)

95-96 AD - Others believe this to be the date the letter was written. If so, the letter tells of events to come later; but why did John not mention the destruction of the Temple and the fall of Jerusalem? Believed mostly from statement by Irenaeus.

Both sides believe they have proof to back up their beliefs. The understanding one has will dictate his teaching, not only of the letter of Revelation, but other letters as well.

I Sam. 17:43-51; II Chron. 24:17-25
Ps. 33:12ff; 44:1-3; 118:8-9; Prov. 21:31
Isa. 31:1-3; Jer. 17:5-8; 37:6-10; Hos. 10:13-15

"...You are mistaken, not knowing the Scriptures nor the power of God." Mt. 22:29 (NKJV)

SPECIAL STUDY: WHAT SAVES US?

Acts 2:36-37; 16:27-30
(Partly by Don Earl Boatman and partly by Daniel S. Merritt)

INTRO.

There are many teachings in Scripture that are important to us in this life. Some have temporal effects and others have eternal effects.

The most important is SALVATION! Although most folks do not believe it; observable by their actions.

There are several Persons, events, and actions that the Scripture, the Word of God states that save us. Therefore, it seems to me, imperative that every person look in the Word of God to determine just how it answers the question, "What must I do to be saved?"

There are many opinions concerning salvation, some are:

1. Everyone will eventually be saved. because God is a God of love, and would not commit anyone to hell forever.
2. Just be sincere, and do the best you can.
3. Only believe, or just have faith only. With that some say you can never be lost, while others say one can be lost.
4. Others believe that God has already decided who is going to be saved, and there is nothing one can do.
5. Same say one must be baptized to be saved. In that, some believe sprinkling, pouring, or immersion is the way.

6. Still others say that baptism is not water baptism, but Holy Spirit baptism.

7. And there are other teachings stating HOW.

I believe that the ONLY way to be sure is to scour God's Word, searching to find the answer. You cannot find the answer in any other place. The Bible ALONE has the answer of how to be saved, how to make it to Heaven.

I also believe that everything the Bible says to do for salvation, we must do.

Put opinions aside. Daddy, Mama, preachers, teachers (including me), and all others are not the authority. ONLY the Word of God is the authority.

The phrases: *faith only, baptism only, Jesus only, repentance only, belief only,* & the like for salvation, are nowhere found in Scripture.

We should always be careful using words like: only, always, every, and alone. Not just with salvation, but dealing with any topic.

Let's look at what God, through the Holy Spirit, through Bible writers has to say concerning, "How must I be saved?"

I - GOD SAVES US

I Tim. 1:1, 2:3, 4:10; Heb. 11:6 – Since the word *ONLY* does not appear, we can safely assume that there is more to salvation.

II - CHRIST SAVES US

We hear this statement a lot - Mt. 1:21; Lk. 2:11; John 1:29; 14:6. Again, the word ONLY does not appear. God the Father, and God the Son both save us.

III - WE ARE SAVED BY CHRIST'S LIFE

There is a difference between Christ & Christ's life - Rom. 5:10; Cor. 15:17; Heb. 7:25. His life, His actions save us, and He continues making intercession for us. We are saved not only by Christ, Christ's life, but also:

IV - WE ARE SAVED BY CHRIST'S BLOOD

Rom. 5:8-9; Eph. 1:7; Heb. 9:22 – If we had used the word *ONLY* beside either one of these, then we would be anti-Scriptural, and be making up our own doctrine. Another familiar phrase in the Bible is:

V - WE ARE SAVED BY GRACE

So we must add that to our list. Rom. 3:23-24; Eph. 2:8; Titus 2:11 – None of us are perfect. We all need God's grace to be saved. If we lived a perfect life, then we would not need grace.

VI - WE ARE ALSO SAVED BY THE GOSPEL

Rom. 1:16; I Cor. 1:18, 21; I Cor. 15:1-4 – Did you know there were so many Persons, actions, and events that save us? And nowhere have we seen the word *ONLY*! The world needs to hear the Gospel, the good news about Christ's death, burial, and resurrection.

VII - SAVED BY CALLING ON THE NAME OF THE LORD

This one you may have heard; we are saved by calling on His name (Rom. 10:13). This is not the whole picture, so more is required.

VIII - WE ARE SAVED BY WORDS

How can words save us? Let's see. Acts 11:14; Heb. 4:12; Js. 1:21. Words are powerful; the words of God created the earth and universe, and even save us. When we use the words *ONLY* or *ALONE*, we must always be careful.

IX - WE ARE SAVED BY HOPE

Rom. 8:24; I Pet. 1:3 – If the Scripture said "hope only", then many would be happy, because they hope they are going to Heaven, that God is not really going to send anyone to hell.

X - SAVED BY CONFESSION

This we have heard often, that we must confess Jesus as the Christ, the Messiah (Mt. 10:32; Rom. 10:9; Jn. 8:24) This leaves out JW's, Mormons, Jews, Moslems, all who do not confess Jesus as the Christ, that Jesus is God (Is. 9:6).

XI - SAVED BY REPENTANCE

Scripture talks about repentance as saving and taking away sins. Most agree on this (Acts 3:19; 8:22; 17:30). So far, we have not placed any one of these doctrines above another. They are all important, all necessary for salvation, and not one can be done away with. But one doctrine that many would like to see taken out of the Bible is that we are:

XII - SAVED BY REMAINING FAIHFUL

A most unpopular doctrine; but Scripture states we are saved by being faithful, for neglect will cause us to be lost (Mt. 10:22; I Cor. 9:27; 15:1-2; II Tim. 2:12-13; Rev. 2:10). The Jews knew this, & folks like the Pharisees kept this as a ritual They kept the letter of the law, but not the spirit of the law. Since Jesus came, He demands a righteousness that exceeds that of the Pharisees. That means that if we want to make it to Heaven, we must remain faithful (II Pet. 2:20-22).

XIII - SAVED BY FAITH

This is one in which many delight. I know many who believe this. They use the words 'faith *only* or faith *alone'*. But, this is an anti-scriptural doctrine, and there is no salvation in it.

However, it Is most certainly a part of salvation, and no one can be saved without faith (Acts 16:31; Rom. 5:1; Gal. 3:26; Heb. 10:39). The words *faith* and *only* are used together only one time in all of Scripture, and that is in James 2:24 where the Bible teaches salvation is *not* by faith only—the exact opposite of the 'faith only' teaching. Luther, Zwingli, and Calvin taught the anti-biblical doctrine of faith only.

XIV – SAVED BY WORKS

This is taught is *some* churches today, while others say works have nothing to do with salvation. Again, let's appeal to Scripture. Mt. 7:21; I Tim 3:16; James 2:17-26; I Jn. 2:3-6. There must be a proper balance between faith and works. Scripture does not say works only, but faith *and* works.

XV - SAVED BY IMMERSION (BAPTISM)

Some say immersion has nothing to do with salvation; however, Jesus, Peter, John, Philip, Ananias, and others say it does.

Acts 2:38 – When the people asked, 'What shall we do?' Why did Peter not respond by saying only believe? He did not even use the words, faith or believe, because they already had faith. What they needed to do was repent, and be immersed. Different versions say the same thing.

Acts 22:16 – Ryrie says in footnote to his study Bible that baptism does not wash away sins; who are we to believe: Ryrie or the Bible?

See also Rom. 6:3-9; Acts 8, 9, 10, 16; Gal. 3:27. Again, nowhere in Scripture that says we are saved by immersion (baptism) *only*. That would be anti-scriptural.

XVI - SAVE YOURSELVES

Phil. 2:12 – But we cannot save ourselves by *ourselves only*. There is God's part and our part.

CONCL.

All these combine to enable a person to be saved. We do not have the option to select one, two, or three. It is neither faith *only*, immersion *only*, repentance *only*, nor any of the others *only*, but taken together.

Scripture also speaks of sacrifice and obedience, saving one another and women being saved through child bearing; bearing fruit or else be cut down and burned. Then Paul says in I Corinthians 13:1-3 that without love, everything else we do is worthless. (see also Jn. 13:34-35).

So, there is a lot involved in salvation. Actually it boils down to obedience: Jn. 14:15, 21, 23; 15:10,14. Whatever Jesus says to do, we must do. I believe it is most unwise to believe what my dad, mom, preacher, a book, or anyone else says, without checking what Jesus says. He is the authority. The church in Berea Acts 17:11, did not believe what Paul said, but 'searched the Scriptures daily to find out whether Paul's teachings were true.'

Place your salvation only in Jesus and His Word. If you have not complied with His teachings, then you are urged to do so, by being obedient to Jesus today.

Then Simon Peter answered Him, "Lord, to whom shall we go? You have the words to eternal life...." Jn. 6:68 (NKJV)

QUESTION 1:
WHAT SHOULD A CHRISTIAN'S ATTITUDE BE TOWARD ENEMIES?

- Ex. 19:17-18 – Love enemies
- Daniel 1-3 – Daniel, Hananiah, Mishael, & Azariah served enemy faithfully
- Ezra & Nehemiah served enemy faithfully
- Job 9:12 – Do not question God, but obey
- Job 31:28-30 – Do not rejoice at destruction of enemy
- Prov. 24:17-18 – Do not rejoice when enemy falls or stumbles
- Ez. 18:21ff – Wicked turns from sins...shall live (as Nebuchadnezzar and Manasseh) fair or not?
- Ez. 33:11, 17, 20, & 31 – God has no pleasure in the death of the wicked. Should we?
- Jer. 19:7 – Pray for enemies
- Mt. 5:43-48 – Love enemies, bless, pray, & do good to them
- Mt. 7:21-23 - God knows only the obedient
- Lk. 6:27-31 – Same as above
- Lk. 6:46 – Don't call Jesus Lord if not going to obey Him
- Rom. 12:9ff – Bless those who persecute you
- Rom. 13:1-7 – Obey authorities
- Gal. 3:8ff – Only faithful Jews and Gentiles are sons of Abraham
- Ph. 2:13-16 – Be lights to crooked & perverse generation – to win them to Christ
- I Thes. 5:14-22 – Do not render evil for evil
- I Tim. 2:1-7 – Pray for all men, including kings, & those in authority
- Titus 3:1-8 – Obey authorities, speak evil of no one
- I Pet. 2:12ff – Obey kings and authorities
- I Pet. 3:9ff – Do not return evil for evil
- II Pet. 2:10-11 – Do not speak evil of dignitaries
- II Pet. 3:9 – God wants all to come to repentance

A Thought To Remember

George G. Williams maintains that from 70 to 78% of words used by W. Somerset Maughn, Sinclair Lewis, R. L. Stephenson, and Charles Dickens have only one syllable; as do: 80% of I Cor. 13, 73% of Ps. 23, and 76% of the model prayer. "Speak," said Abraham Lincoln, "so the most lowly can understand you, and the rest will have no difficulty."

QUESTION 2:
FINAL COMING OR FALL OF JERUSALEM?

Do these Scriptures refer to the final coming of Jesus, **OR** do they refer to the fall of Jerusalem (A.D. 67-70) and the end of the Jewish nation? Some of these Scriptures are examples.

- Gen. 41:1-4, 32 – God would shortly bring it to pass
- Gen. 49:1, 10 – in the last days; until Shiloh (Jesus) comes
- Isaiah 2:1-2
- Isaiah 13:1-6, 10 – day of Lord at hand; similar to Mt. 24
- Jer. 43:10 God uses pagans to destroy
- Joel 1:15; 2:1, 10-11, 28f; 3:1, 14 – day of Lord at hand
- Zep. 1:7 – day of Lord at hand; 14 – day of the Lord is near
- Mt. 3:2; 4:17 – Kingdom of Heaven at hand
- Mt. 16 – some here will see Son of Man coming in His Kingdom
- Mt. 24, (34); Mk. 13; Lk. 21 – this generation (temple destroyed; end of Jewish nation, AD 70
- Acts 2:16-21 – in the last days; (Isaiah 13:10; Mt. 24:29)
- Rom. 16:20 – crush Satan shortly
- I Cor. 7:29; 10:11 – time is short; end of ages have come
- Phil. 4:5 – Lord is at hand
- Col. 1:6, 23 – Gospel preached to all the world; every creature
- Rom: 16:26 – Scripture made known to all nations (Roman world?) (Lk. 2:1) Acts 1:8
- I Thes. 4:15 – we who are alive and remain at the coming of the Lord

- II Tim. 3:1 – in the last days
- Heb. 1:2 – God…has in these last days spoken to us by His Son
- Heb. 9:26 – end of ages …put away sin by the sacrifice of Himself
- James 5:8-9 – coming of the Lord is at hand; judge standing at door
- I Pet. 1:20 – manifest in these last times for you
- I Pet. 4:17 – time has come for judgment to begin
- II Pet. 1:14 – Shortly (example)
- I John 2:18 – it is the last hour
- Jude 18 – mockers in the last time
- Rev. 1:1; 22:6 – things which must shortly take place
- Rev. 1:3 – time is near; 22:10

QUESTION 3:
WILL THE EARTH BE DESTROYED OR RENEWED? WILL HEAVEN BE ON EARTH?

- Gen. 6:13 – I will destroy them (all flesh) with the earth
- Gen. 7:4; 9:11 – destroy all living things; flood to destroy earth
- Psalm 37:9, 11, 22, 29-34 – those who wait, the meek, and the blessed will inherit the earth forever
- Psalm 93:2 – world established, cannot be moved
- Psalm 102:25-28 – work of Your hands will perish…You will change hem
- Psalm 104:5 – earth should not be moved forever
- Eccl. 1:4 – earth abides forever
- Zec. 2:10ff; Jn. 1:11ff;
- Mt. 5:5, 18 – meek inherit the earth; pass away or changed?
- I Cor. 7:31 – for the form of this world is passing away
- Gal. 3:7ff.
- Heb. 1:10-12 – Heaven and earth will perish…they will be changed
- II Pet. 3:6-10 – world perished by water…earth and works burned up—totally destroyed or changed?

- Rev. 6:10 -- made us kings and priests...we shall reign on the earth
- Rev. 21:1-3, 10, 25 – New Jerusalem coming down out of Heaven...Tabernacle of God is with men, and He will dwell with them; holy Jerusalem descending out of Heaven from God; its gates shall not be shut (why have gates?)

Just thought I would ask.

Cannot Have God the Father Without Having God the Son

Mt. 11:27; Jn. 3:16-18, 35-36; 5:23-ff;
I Jn. 2:22-25; 4:7-16; 5:10-23; II Jn. 9-11

QUESTION 4:
WHO ARE THE NEW ISRAEL?

- Mt. 21:43 – Taken from Jews and given to Gentiles
- Mt. 12:46-50 – All who do the Father's will
- Lk. 2:10, 31-32 – All people, Jew and Gentile
- Acts 10: 34-36; 15:13-18 – Gentiles as well as Jews; 13:42-52
- Rom. 2:28ff – Jew inwardly, not outwardly
- Rom. 10:12-13 – Whoever calls on the name of the Lord (See also 2:28-29)
- Rom. 11:1-24 – Unbelieving Jews cut off; believing Gentiles grafted in; he who repents grafted in again
- I Cor. 12:13 – All immersed into one body, Jews and Greeks
- Gal. 3:7, 26-29 – Sons of Abraham only by faith; immersed into Christ, put on Christ
- Gal. 6:15-16 - Circumcision nor uncircumcision mean anything, but those who walk after Jesus Christ
- Eph. 2:11 - 3:21 – By faith Jew and Gentile have access to God
- Ph. 3:2-3 – True circumcision who worship God in the Spirit
- Co. 3:11 – To circumcised and uncircumcised Christ is all in all.

Special Study:
Obedience and Disobedience

- **Gen.** 2:15-17 - God gave commands to Adam and Eve
- **Gen.** 4:1-7; I Jn. 3:12 – Cain did evil by not obeying God
- **Gen.** 6:22 – Noah followed God's commands
- **Gen.** 12:1-3; 17:1-9; 22:1-2, 15-18; Heb. 11:8-9; Js. 2:20-24 –
- Abraham obeyed God, keeping His commandments
- **Deut.** 6; 8; 10:12-14; 11:13, 22, 26-28; 12:32; 30:10 – God to
- Israel under Moses
- **Jos.** 1:7-9, 16-18; 8:35 – God to Israel under Joshua
- **I Sam.** 2:27-36 – God condemns Eli for not being obedient
- **I Sam.** 12:14-15 – Samuel to Israel
- **I Sam.** 15:22-23 – Samuel to Saul
- **I Kings** 2:1-5 – David to Solomon
- **I Kings** 3:14; 6:12; 9:2-9; II Chron. 7:17-22 – God to Solomon
- **Deut.** 17:14-20 – Moses concerning a king – they disobeyed – I
  Kings 11:1-13; I Chron. 3:1-9; II Chron. 1:13-17; 9:13-28

There are many Scriptures in the Old Testament concerning obedience and disobedience, and the results.

- **Matt.** 5:20-22, 27-28, 31-48; 7:21-27; 12:50; 22:37-40
- John 7:17; 14:15, 23, 31; 15:1-15
- Rom. 1:29-31; 4:1-8; 5:1-2; 11:1-24; 12:1-2; 13:1-14
- I Cor. 6:9-11
- Gal. 5:1-7, 18
- Eph. 4:28
- Ph. 2:14-16
- Heb. 10:19-29
- Js. 2:14-26
- I Jn. 2:3-6; 3:22-24; 5:1-3
- Rev. 22:14

See Special Study, "What Saves Us?" There are many other teachings of Jesus, and other writers of the New Testament, that we are to obey in order to please God and to receive forgiveness of sins.

SPECIAL STUDY:
IS JESUS GOD?

There are different ideas of who Jesus of Nazareth is. As usual, the best way to determine this is to study the Holy Bible to find the answer. There are many Scriptures that prove that Jesus is God. Descriptions of the Father and the Son are compared below.

JEHOVAH	SCRIPTURE	JESUS	SCRIPTURE
Almighty	Gen. 17:1	Almighty	Rev. 1:8
Alpha/Omega	Rev. 21:6-7	Alpha/Omega	Rev. 1:8
First & Last	Is. 44:6	First & Last	Rev. 22:13
Father	Mt. 6:9	Father	Is. 9:6
Giver of spiritual water	Is. 55:1	Giver of living water	Jn. 4:10-14
Horn of Salvation	Ps. 18:2	Horn of Salvation	Lk. 1:69
Holy One	Is. 12:6	Holy One	Acts 2:27
I AM	Ex. 3:14	I AM	Jn. 8:58
Just God	Is. 45:21	Just One	Acts 7:52
Judge	Is. 33:22	Judge	Acts 10:42
King of Glory	Ps. 24:7-10	Lord of Glory	I Cor. 2:8
King of Israel	Is. 44:6	King of Israel	Jn. 1:49
Lawgiver	Is. 33:22	Mediator of New Covenant	Heb. 9:15
Lord of lords	Ps. 136:3	Lord of Lords	Rev. 19:16
Light	Ps. 27:1	Light	Jn. 1:4-9
Only Creator	Is. 48:13	Only Creator	Col. 1:16
Only Savior	Is. 43:11	God and Savior	Titus 2:13
Peace	Rom. 15:33	Peace	Eph. 2:14
Redeemer	Is. 54:5	Redeemer	Gal. 3:13
Rock	Ps. 18:2	Rock	I Cor. 10:4
Salvation	Is. 12:2	Salvation	Acts 4:12
Shepherd	Is. 40:10-11	Shepherd	Heb.13:20

See also: Isa. 9:6; Col. 2:9; Jn. 2:19-22 (Rom. 6:4); 10:30; 14:9; 14:14 (15:16); Jn. 12:32 (6:44); Jn. 14:3 (I Jn. 3:1-2). This is not all.
(Partly copied)

SPECIAL STUDY:
RIGHTLY DIVIDING THE SCRIPTURES

The Holy Bible is not just one book, but a book of 66 books. They were written over a period of about 1500 years, by about 40 men from different walks of life, from shepherds to kings.

Scripture tells us that the writers were under the inspiration of God. **II Tim. 3:13-17 and II Pet. 1:19-21.** The Bible came from God, not man. We are to study to show ourselves approved to God, and the Scriptures through faith in Christ will make us complete. **Jn. 20:31.**

There are two Testaments or divisions.

The Old Testament has 39 books:

- 5 books of Law – covering the creation, Adam, Eve, Enock, Noah, Abraham (whom God called to begin a special people for Himself –Israelites/Hebrews. – later Jews). Then God using Moses, leads the Hebrews out of captivity in Egypt, and events of their wandering in the wilderness, going to the Promised Land.
- 12 books of History with Joshua, conquering of the promised land, the judges, the three major kings, and the dividing of the kingdom into two kingdoms. Several books concern certain people, and many events of God's dealing with His people.
- 5 books called poetry dealing with Job, Psalms and Proverbs.
- 17 books of Prophecy teaching how God sent men to turn the hearts of the people back to Him.

The New Testament has 27 books:

- 4 books called the Gospels of Christ, from the birth of Jesus, His life, His teachings, choosing 12 men called apostles to carry on His teachings, His death, burial, and resurrection.
- 1 book of History, which tells of the beginnings of the Church, how people became a part of that church, and how it spread to the world.
- 21 books called letters, written to congregations and to certain men. These give us truths of living the Christian life.
- 1 book of prophecy. Many believe these prophecies are still in the future, while many believe much of the prophecies were fulfilled in AD 70 when the Jews ceased to be a nation, and the temple destroyed. Christians are now God's chosen people *Gal. 3:7.*

SPECIAL STUDY: THE CHRISTIAN LIFE

1. When you thought about becoming a Christian, what questions did you ask, and/or what questions were asked you?
2. II - What does it mean to be a Christian?
3. III - How has your life changed?
4. IV - A lot is involved in being a Christian:
   a. Acts 2:42
      i. Apostles Doctrine
         1. II Timothy 3:16-17
         2. II Timothy 2:15
         3. Ephesians 6:1-3
         4. Revelation 21:1-8 – Hell is forever, as is Heaven
         5. John 15:1-11; Galatians 5:22-26
         6. I John 2:3-6
         7. John 13:34-35
         8. Matthew 5:43-48
         9. Matthew 22:37-40

   ii.   Fellowship
1. Hebrews 10:22-125
2. Philippians 2:1-4, 14

  iii.   Breaking of Bread
1. Mark 14:22-25 – Jesus instituting the Lord's Supper
2. I Corinthians 11:23-30 – Paul repeating what Jesus said, giving more information
3. Acts 20:7

  iv.   Prayers
1. Philippians 4:6; 1:1-7
2. I Thessalonians 5:17-18
3. Luke 6:12

Conclusion: Being a Christian is serious business. We must be trying to obey His commandments; loving God, our neighbors, and our enemies, Matthew 5:43-48.

SPECIAL STUDY:
LISTS OF SINS

Rom. 1:29-31	I Cor. 6:9-10	Gal. 5:19-21
Filled with all sexual immorality	fornicators	works of flesh
wickedness	adulterers	fornication
covetousness	homosexuals	uncleanness
maliciousness (evil)	sodomites	lewdness
full of envy	thieves	idolatry
murder	covetous	sorcery
strife (quarrelsome)	drunkards	hatred
deceit	revilers	contentions
evil-mindedness	extortioners	jealousies
whisperers	unrighteous	outburst of wrath
backbiters	will not inherit the kingdom of God	selfish ambitions
haters of God		dissensions
violent		heresies
proud		envy
boasters		murders
inventors of evil things		drunkenness
disobedient to parents		revelries
undiscerning		will not inherit the Kingdom of God
Untrustworthy		
unloving		
unforgiving		
Unmerciful		
all deserving of death – those approving and suppressing the truth		See also 1 Cor 5:9-13; 6:11; Eph. 5:1-7, 18; Rom. 13:1-10

Col. 3:5-9	I Pet. 4:2-3	Rev. 21:8
anger	lewdness	cowardly
wrath	lusts	unbelieving
malice	drunkenness	abominable
blasphemy	revelries	murderers
filthy language	drinking parties	sexual immoral
lying	abominable idolatries	sorcerers
		idolaters
		have part in lake which burns with fire and brimstone which is the second death.
See also: II Tim. 2:22-23; 3:1-8; I Pet. 2:13ff		

DAILY BIBLE READING

Daily Bible reading is important to Christians, as we seek to know all we can about our God, His Son Jesus Christ, and Their will for us. There are 1189 chapters in the Bible, 929 in the OT and 260 in the NT. Reading 23 chapters each week, we can easily read through the Bible in one year. Mark each chapter as you read, and take notes of what stands out to you. God bless you in your reading of God's Word.

Old Testament

Genesis 1, 2, 3, 4, 5, 6, 7, 8, 9, 10, 11, 12, 13, 14, 15, 16, 17, 18, 19, 20, 21, 22, 23, 24, 25, 26, 27, 28, 29, 30, 31, 32, 33, 34, 35, 36, 37, 38, 39, 40, 41, 42, 43, 44, 45, 46, 47, 48, 49, 50

Exodus 1, 2, 3, 4, 5, 6, 7, 8, 9, 10, 11, 12, 13, 14, 15, 16, 17, 18, 19, 20, 21, 22, 23, 24, 25, 26, 27, 28, 29, 30, 31, 32, 33, 34, 35, 36, 37, 38, 39, 40

Leviticus 1, 2, 3, 4, 5, 6, 7, 8, 9, 10, 11, 12, 13, 14, 15, 16, 17, 18, 19, 20, 21, 22, 23, 24, 25, 26, 27

Numbers 1, 2, 3, 4, 5, 6, 7, 8, 9, 10, 11, 12, 13, 14, 15, 16, 17, 18, 19, 20, 21, 22, 23, 24, 25, 26, 27, 28, 29, 30, 31, 32, 33, 34, 35, 36

Deuteronomy 1, 2, 3, 4, 5, 6, 7, 8, 9, 10, 11, 12, 13, 14, 15, 16, 17, 18, 19, 20, 21, 22, 23, 24, 25, 26, 27, 28, 29, 30, 31, 32, 33, 34

Joshua 1, 2, 3, 4, 5, 6, 7, 8, 9, 10, 11, 12, 13, 14, 15, 16, 17, 18, 19, 20, 21, 22, 23, 24

Judges 1, 2, 3, 4, 5, 6, 7, 8, 9, 10, 11, 12, 13, 14, 15, 16, 17, 18, 19, 20, 21

Ruth 1, 2, 3, 4

I Samuel 1, 2, 3, 4, 5, 6, 7, 8, 9, 10, 11, 12, 13, 14, 15, 16, 17, 18, 19, 20, 21, 22, 23, 24, 25, 26, 27, 28, 29, 30, 31

II Samuel 1, 2, 3, 4, 5, 6, 7, 8, 9, 10, 11, 12, 13, 14, 15, 16, 17, 18, 19, 20, 21, 22, 23, 24

NOTES:

I Kings 1, 2, 3, 4, 5, 6, 7, 8, 9, 10, 11, 12, 13, 14, 15, 16, 17, 18, 19, 20, 21, 22

II Kings 1, 2, 3, 4, 5, 6, 7, 8, 9, 10, 11, 12, 13, 14, 15, 16, 17, 18, 19, 20, 21, 22, 23, 24, 25

I Chronicles 1, 2, 3, 4, 5, 6, 7, 8, 9, 10, 11, 12, 13, 14, 15, 16, 17, 18, 19, 20, 21, 22, 23, 24, 25, 26, 27, 28, 29

II Chronicles 1, 2, 3, 4, 5, 6, 7, 8, 9, 10, 11, 12, 13, 14, 15, 16, 17, 18, 19, 20, 21, 22, 23, 24, 25, 26, 27, 28, 29, 30, 31, 32, 33, 34, 35, 36

Ezra 1, 2, 3, 4, 5, 6, 7, 8, 9, 10

Nehemiah 1, 2, 3, 4, 5, 6, 7, 8, 9, 10, 11, 12, 13

Esther 1, 2, 3, 4, 5, 6, 7, 8, 9, 10

Job 1, 2, 3, 4, 5, 6, 7, 8, 9, 10, 11, 12, 13, 14, 15, 16, 17, 18, 19, 20, 21, 22, 23, 24, 25, 26, 27, 28, 29, 30, 31, 32, 33, 34, 35, 36, 37, 38, 39, 40, 41, 42

Psalms 1, 2, 3, 4, 5, 6, 7, 8, 9, 10, 11, 12, 13, 14, 15, 16, 17, 18, 19, 20, 21, 22, 23, 24, 25, 26, 27, 28, 29, 30, 31, 32, 33, 34, 35, 36, 37, 38, 39, 40, 41, 42, 43, 44, 45, 46, 47, 48, 49, 50, 51, 52, 53, 54, 55, 56, 57, 58, 59, 60, 61, 62, 63, 64, 65, 66, 67, 68, 69, 70, 71, 72, 73, 74, 75, 76, 77, 78, 79, 80, 81, 82, 83, 84, 85, 86, 87, 88, 89, 90, 91, 92, 93, 94, 95, 96, 97, 98, 99, 100, 101, 102, 103, 104, 105, 106, 107, 108, 109, 110, 111, 112, 113, 114, 115, 116, 117, 118, 119, 120, 121, 122, 123, 124, 125, 126, 127, 128, 129, 130, 131, 132, 133, 134, 135, 136, 137, 138, 139, 140, 141, 142, 143, 144, 145, 146, 147, 148, 149, 150

Proverbs 1, 2, 3, 4, 5, 6, 7, 8, 9, 10, 11, 12, 13, 14, 15, 16, 17, 18, 19, 20, 21, 22, 23, 24, 25, 26, 27, 28, 29, 30, 31

Ecclesiastes 1, 2, 3, 4, 5, 6, 7, 8, 9, 10, 11, 12

Song of Solomon 1, 2, 3, 4, 5, 6, 7, 8

NOTES:

Isaiah 1, 2, 3, 4, 5, 6, 7, 8, 9, 10, 11, 12, 13, 14, 15, 16, 17, 18, 19, 20, 21, 22, 23, 24, 25, 26, 27, 28, 29, 30, 31, 32, 33, 34, 35, 36, 37, 38, 39, 40, 41, 42, 43, 44, 45, 46, 47, 48, 49, 50, 51, 52, 53, 54, 55, 56, 57, 58, 59, 60, 61, 62, 63, 64, 65, 66

Jeremiah 1, 2, 3, 4, 5, 6, 7, 8, 9, 10, 11, 12, 13, 14, 15, 16, 17, 18, 19, 20, 21, 22, 23, 24, 25, 26, 27, 28, 29, 30, 31, 32, 33, 34, 35, 36, 37, 38, 39, 40, 41, 42, 43, 44, 45, 46, 47, 48, 49, 50, 51, 52

Lamentations 1, 2, 3, 4, 5

Ezekiel 1, 2, 3, 4, 5, 6, 7, 8, 9, 10, 11, 12, 13, 14, 15, 16, 17, 18, 19, 20, 21, 22, 23, 24, 25, 26, 27, 28, 29, 30, 31, 32, 33, 34, 35, 36, 37, 38, 39, 40, 41, 42, 43, 44, 45, 46, 47, 48

Daniel 1, 2, 3, 4, 5, 6, 7, 8, 9, 10, 11, 12

Hosea 1, 2, 3, 4, 5, 6, 7, 8, 9, 10, 11, 12, 13, 14

Joel 1, 2, 3

Amos 1, 2, 3, 4, 5, 6, 7, 8, 9

Obadiah 1

Jonah 1, 2, 3, 4

Micah 1, 2, 3, 4, 5, 6, 7

Nahum 1, 2, 3

Habakkuk 1, 2, 3

Zephaniah 1, 2, 3

Haggai 1, 2

Zechariah 1, 2, 3, 4, 5, 6, 7, 8, 9, 10, 11, 12, 13, 14

Malachi 1, 2, 3, 4

NOTES:

New Testament

Matthew 1, 2, 3, 4, 5, 6, 7, 8, 9, 10, 11, 12, 13, 14, 15, 16, 17, 18, 19, 20, 21, 22, 23, 24, 25, 26, 27, 28

Mark 1, 2, 3, 4, 5, 6, 7, 8, 9, 10, 11, 12, 13, 14, 15, 16

Luke 1, 2, 3, 4, 5, 6, 7, 8, 9, 10, 11, 12, 13, 14, 15, 16, 17, 18, 19, 20, 21, 22, 23, 24

John 1, 2, 3, 4, 5, 6, 7, 8, 9, 10, 11, 12, 13, 14, 15, 16, 17, 18, 19, 20, 21

Acts 1, 2, 3, 4, 5, 6, 7, 8, 9, 10, 11, 12, 13, 14, 15, 16, 17, 18, 19, 20, 21, 22, 23, 24, 25, 26, 27, 28

Romans 1, 2, 3, 4, 5, 6, 7, 8, 9, 10, 11, 12, 13, 14, 15, 16

I Corinthians 1, 2, 3, 4, 5, 6, 7, 8, 9, 10, 11, 12, 13, 14, 15, 16

II Corinthians 1, 2, 3, 4, 5, 6, 7, 8, 9, 10, 11, 12, 13

Galatians 1, 2, 3, 4, 5, 6　　　　**Ephesians** 1, 2, 3, 4, 5, 6

Philippians 1, 2, 3, 4　　　　**Colossians** 1, 2, 3, 4

I Thessalonians 1, 2, 3, 4, 5　　　　**II Thessalonians** 1, 2, 3

I Timothy 1, 2, 3, 4, 5, 6　　**II Timothy** 1, 2, 3, 4　**Titus** 1, 2, 3

Philemon 1　　　**Hebrews** 1, 2, 3, 4, 5, 6, 7, 8, 9, 10, 11, 12, 13

James 1, 2, 3, 4, 5　**I Peter** 1, 2, 3, 4, 5　**II Peter** 1, 2, 3

I John 1, 2, 3, 4, 5　　**II John** 1　　**III John** 1　　**Jude** 1

Revelation 1, 2, 3, 4, 5, 6, 7, 8, 9, 10, 11, 12, 13, 14, 15, 16, 17, 18, 19, 20, 21, 22

NOTES:

NOTES:

NOTES:

Delightful Bible Reading

The Method

1 Approach it as the Word of God Psalm 119:128
2 Read with a love for truth,
and a desire to know it Psalm 119:72
3 Read with a will to obey Psalm 119:33-34
4 Have a special time for
Bible reading Psalm 119:147-148
5 Ask God for enlightenment Psalm 119:18
6 Read expectantly Psalm 119:7
7 Meditate on what you read Psalm 119:15
8 Commit it to memory Psalm 119:11
9 Read with a view to teaching others Psalm 119:46

The Blessings

1 Enjoyment of God's Word Psalm 119:103
2 Wisdom Psalm 119:98-100
3 Reason for our faith Psalm 119:42
4 Light for living Psalm 119:105
5 Defense against temptation Psalm 119:11
6 Strength and comfort Psalm 119:50
7 Peace Psalm 119:165
8 Salvation Psalm 119:41
9 The happy fellowship of other
Bible readers Psalm 119:63

by: Lawrence W. Merritt

www.ingramcontent.com/pod-product-compliance
Lightning Source LLC
Chambersburg PA
CBHW070945120626
46546CB00004B/1577